Entrepreneur Mind

The Ten Golden Entrepreneurial Success
and Financial Wealth

Business Startup lessons from Steve Jobs, Bill Gates, Jeff Bezos, Elon Musk, Arianna Huffington, Sir Richard Branson, and Tony Robbins

*

A. J. PARR

*

GRAPEVINE BOOKS
FIRST EDITION
2019

ALL RIGHTS RESERVED – FAIR USE

All Rights Reserved under Title 17, U.S. Code, International and Pan-American Copyright Conventions. The sharing, duplication, distribution, uploading, or transfer of this electronic book by any digital or printed means without explicit permission of the publisher is unauthorized.

DISCLAIMER: The 1976 Copyright Act (Section 107) states that "fair use" is permitted when writing criticism, comments, news reports, and didactic texts (otherwise infringing). Non-profit, educational or personal use favor fair use. Napoleon Hill quotes taken from the 1937 edition of "Think and Grow Rich" presently in the Public Domain

AUTHOR: A.J. Parr

PUBLISHED BY: Grapevine Books (Ediciones De La Parra)

edicionesdelaparra@gmail.com

Copyright © 2019 Grapevine Books/Ediciones De La Parra. All Rights Reserved.

ISBN: 9781095003213

CONTENT

FOREWORD

Page 1

RULE 1 - **HEED THE LESSONS OF FAILURE**

Page 9

RULE 2 - **ALWAYS RISE AFTER YOU FALL**

Page 17

RULE 3 - **PERSIST UNTIL YOU SUCCEED**

Page 23

RULE 4 - **YOU ARE THE FORGER OF YOUR DESTINY**

Page 31

RULE 5 - **GRASP THE POWER OF THE UNCONSCIOUS**

Page 39

RULE 6 - **OBSERVE YOUR THINKING PATTERNS**

Page 51

RULE 7 - **MAKE YOUR AFFIRMATIONS A HABIT**

Page 63

RULE 8 - **ESCAPE FROM NEGATIVE THINKING**

Page 73

RULE 9 – **DISCOVER THE POWER OF MEDITATION**

Page 77

RULE 10 - **DEVELOP A WINNING MINDSET**

Page 87

FOREWORD

"It's fine to celebrate success, but it is more important to heed the lessons of failure."

Bill Gates

A. J. PARR

DO YOU SEEK ENTREPRENEURIAL SUCCESS but don't know how to develop a winning mindset? Are you facing failure and need help? Are you somehow "stuck" in life and cannot find the road to your personal and business growth? Do you wish to succed, ultimately conquering financial freedom and wealth?

This precious little guide presents *The Ten Golden Rules of Entrepreneurial Success and Financial Wealth* employed by some of the world's wealthiest entrepreneurs, including Steve Jobs (Apple), Bill Gates (Microsoft), Jeff Bezos (Amazon), Elon Musk (Tesla), Arianna Huffington (The Huffington Post), Richard Branson (Virgin)and Tony Robbins, among others. It contains the vital teachings, essential beliefs, habits and visions that allowed these successful entrepreneurs to turn their initial failures into undisputed success and meet financial wealth.

Its inspiring and revealing chapters are packed with valuable lessons, including:

Among other priced lessons, you will learn:

How to develop the winning mindset of the rich and famous

*The secret formula that turns failure into success

*The mysterious force that forges your destiny

*The hidden importance of your thinking patterns

*How to make your unconscious work for you and your business

*Understanding creativity and unleashing its power

*How to deal with negative thoughts and obstacles

*The secret power of Affirmations

*How the rich and famous grew their business from scratch.

*And more!

GENESIS OF THESE GOLDEN RULES

About a decade ago, I had no business, no job, no life project and, last but not least, almost no savings. And, like most aspiring entrepreneurs, my first attempts to create a profitable business had blatantly failed.

But I did not give up. I was doing something wrong. But what?

Hoping for an answer, I studied the careers of some of the world's richest and most successful entrepreneurs. How did these and other successful businessmen and women manage to rightly face and overcome failure? What drove them to their ultimate recovery and allowed them to meet success finally? Was it predestination? To what degree had mere fate or destiny play a role in their triumphs? ¿Or was it only luck or good fortune?

Hoping to find if there was a secret formula for success or not, I found the common denominators and applied them to develop a winning mindset and build a successful new business from scratch.

Those of you who have personally met me know that I presently make a living from my online business, in the comfort of my home, without imposed schedules or bosses. It took several years. But, I would have never made it without intensive research, and by applying what I have called *The Ten Golden Rules of Entrepreneurial Success and Financial Wealth,* conveniently laid out for you in this new book.

IMPORTANCE OF A WINNING MINDSET

Throughout this last decade, I have noticed that a winning mindset is vital for success. Not only my own case, but also in those of countless successful entrepreneurs.

However, to develop a winning mindset you first need to understand the basics of how your mind works, observe your thinking patterns and notice how they influence you, and how only the right affirmations and attitudes can make you think and behave like a winner, boosting your inner confidence and strength, as well of your chances of conquering entrepreneurial success and wealth.

Developing a winning mindset is the essence of the following chapters, which intend to stimulate your inner transformation and impel the winning attitude you need.

Successful entrepreneurs like what they do and do what they like. They have no boss, no boring schedule, can take time off whenever they need, can travel the world, and enjoy more free time that you can imagine.

If that is what you want, you can get there if you try. But you must follow a set of basic and simple rules and prepare yourself if you truly aspire to reach the top. These will not turn you into an overnight millionaire. But they can help you gain financial freedom and leave the rat race, allowing you to never have to hold a 9-to-5 job or wrestle with a boss anymore, managing you own time and responsibilities, and enjoying a more pleasing, peaceful, and rewarding life.

If you too want to develop a winning mindset, then read on and start your journey today!

A. J. PARR

RULE 1.- HEED THE LESSONS OF FAILURE

"It is only through failure that we learn. Many of the world's finest minds have learned this the hard way."

Richard Branson

A. J. PARR

STARTING OUT A NEW BUSINESS IS NO EASY TASK. And, perhaps the hardest part for many consists in having to face multiple failures before meeting success.

If you presently have a job but dream with one day leaving the rat race, entrepreneurship is the way to go. It not only offers financial freedom, but also a higher income than those generated with a steady job.

The main problem is that most newbies quit when meeting their first failures, while successful entrepreneurs believe that failure, in itself, is not a bad thing. The actually sustain that it is actually good, coinciding with the ancient Chinese philosopher Lao Tzu, who over two thousand years ago defined failure as *"the foundation of success, and the means by which it is achieved."*

Success can be defined as *"the ability to achieve a specific goal following a definite plan"*. All in all, success also involves the ability of facing failure with optimism and of learning from each failure. But these are not the only two traits that ultimately separate winners from losers.

Unsuccessful people also tend to make two recurring mistakes: They are always either too meek to chase their dreams or they quit as soon as the first sign of resistance shows up.

In all cases, success takes time and effort and, above all, it requires developing and applying the right mindset that is, the right attitude, way of thinking, mental disposition, or frame of mind.

Launching and running a new business has many ups and downs but it also brings many satisfactions, especially for those who develop the right set of skills and mindset needed for success.

Due to the elevated risks involved in launching a start-up business, many fail to survive their first six months, primarily due to bad business decisions based on inexperience and the lack of marketing skills. However, in a large number of cases, the owners of most startup businesses simply fail because they quit too soon, ignoring that we must learn from each failure if we intend to succeed.

Furthermore, most of these presently recognize the important lessons they learned from their failures and that each mistake brought them a step closer to success.

In fact, as strange as it may sound, failing is often beneficial for it can show us "what works" and "what does not."

TO HEED THE LESSONS OF FAILURE

Years before Bill Gates met financial success, he dropped out of Harvard and co-founded a company called Traf-O-Data, maker of a computer that measured traffic flow. But he lacked experience and funds, so his company soon met bankruptcy. But Gates worked harder than ever on his next project and ultimately founded Microsoft, which was destined to turn him into one of the top billionaires of all times. As he later said:

"It's fine to celebrate success, but it is more important to heed the lessons of failure."

Jeff Bezos is another case. He faced multiple obstacles when he launched the world's first online bookstore. During the first three years of operation, Amazon had zero profits and was on the verge of bankruptcy. People predicted that he would fail. But he knew he was simply ahead of his time and didn't pay any attention to his fiercest detractors. The world was simply not ready for an online bookstore. And time proved him right.

According to Bezos:

"When the world changes around you and when it changes against you, what used to be a tail wind is now a head wind, you have to lean into that and figure out what to do because complaining isn't a strategy."

Before creating WhatsApp, Jan Koum left Yahoo after a ten-year career there and applied for a job at Facebook. But he was blatantly rejected.

Koum had nowhere to turn and no idea of what he would do next. But, he did not give up.

Instead of succumbing to failure, he worked on a new project and thus together with a business partner gave birth to WhatsApp, one of the world's most famous and innovative apps, which he sold in 2014 to Facebook for $22 billion.

As he later concluded:

"A lot of times, people start with a lot of good ideas, but then they don't execute. They lose the purity of their vision. You end up running around in circles."

According to the self-made billionaire Sir Richard Branson, founder of Virgin Group, every person, and especially every entrepreneur, should embrace failure with open arms for it is only through failure that we learn how to succeed:

"If you're an entrepreneur and your first venture wasn't a success, there's no need for the F word (Failure). Learn from it. Pick yourself up. And try; try again."

Branson's experienced many flops. For instance, he faced Virgin Atlantic airline's failure in 1984, Virgin Soda's shut down in 1994 and Virgin's Digital closure in 2007. Even with Virgin records being so big, some of his many musical projects have also gone wrong.

But Branson believes challenges and obstacles are intrinsic elements of the road to success. Regarding failure, he claims it always teaches valuable lessons:

"We don't learn to walk by following rules. We learn by doing and falling over. So don't be embarrassed by your failures, learn from them and start again...

"The most important lesson that I have learned and follow all my life is that we should try and try and try again – but never give up!"

DO WHAT YOU LIKE AND LIKE WHAT YOU DO

Steve Jobs used to say that *"if you don't love it, you're bound to fail..."*

Accordingly, Warren Buffet, whose net worth is $75 billion, states that to succeed, *"you must have a passion for what you do."* He also claimed that *"it is not necessary to do extraordinary things to get extraordinary results."* It is best to work on something you like, but also on what benefits people the most.

CHAPTER HIGHLIGHT

RULE 1: HEED THE LESSONS OF FAILURE

Perhaps the hardest part for many consists in having to face multiple failures before succeeding.

As Sir Richard Branson explains: "If you're an entrepreneur and your first venture wasn't a success, there's no need for the F word (Failure). Learn from it. Pick yourself up. And try; try again."

RULE 2.-ALWAYS RISE AFTER YOU FALL

"I've come to believe that all my past failure and frustration were actually laying the foundation for the understandings that have created the new level of living I now enjoy."

Tony Robbins

A. J. PARR

OVERCOMING PROBLEMS IN LIFE is one of the toughest tasks for most people. We all know that life is tough and that obstacles usually appear when you least expect them. That's what has made characters such as Tony Robbins, among others, so inspirational:

"Problems call us to a higher level – face and solve them now!"

Instead of focusing on your problems, he advices, focus on finding viable solutions:

"Leaders spend five percent of their time on the problem and ninety-five percent of their time on the solution. Get over it & crush it!"

Although Robbins is presently one of the world's most famous and respected life coaches and is followed by countless CEO's, businessmen, politicians and celebrities around the globe, his childhood was what many would call a real nightmare.

Robbins admits being the son of an abusive mother that was an alcoholic and misused prescription drugs. But far from pitying himself and being embarrassed about what he lived, he claims that all the problems he had as a child were the key to his success.

According to Robbins, sometimes the problems and difficulties we find in life are exactly what we need to become the best version of ourselves. This is why he recommends that, instead of being dragged by our circumstances, we should concentrate on *dragging ourselves out* of those same circumstances until we build a winning mindset and grow into what we have decided to be.

LEARN TO RISE AFTER YOU FALL

After interviewing 500 millionaires and successful men of his time, the American author Napoleon Hill concluded in his best-selling book *"Think and Grow Rich,"* that failure only means there is something erroneous with our plan and that we need to fix it.

Among the successful men he interviewed was Henry Ford, who had failed five times as a businessman and was broke before he founded the Ford Motor Company, which turned him into the world's richest man of his time.

As Ford admitted, failure should not be taken as something negative, evil or a strike of bad luck, for, as he wisely sustained, *"failure provides the opportunity to begin again, more intelligently."*

A similar view was shared by his fellow inventor Thomas Edison, also interviewed by Hill, whose first-grade teachers said he was "too stupid to learn anything" and was later fired from his first two jobs for being "non-productive."

Many new entrepreneurs quit when facing failure. But this is wrong. Instead of this, find the cause of the problem and work on a new plan. If you apply the "trial and error" method, then each time something goes wrong, you can always build a new plan and try again.

FINDING A NEW PLAN

When facing failure, most entrepreneurs turn to the method of "trial and error", defined as a heuristic method of problem solving and knowledge acquisition in which a person learns by rejecting strategies that are erroneous in the sense that they do not lead to higher payoffs and instead try out new strategies.

None of the celebrated entrepreneurs mentiones in these chapters would have ever succeeded had they not persisted. And the same goes for you. Do not desist when meeting your first failures. Simply, mend your plan and give it another try.

To those who have experienced failure and do not know what to do, Napoleon Hill recommends immediately working on a new plan, as he expresses in *"Think and Grow Rich"*:

"If your first plan does not work successfully, replace it with another. And if this new plan also fails to work, replace it, in turn, with still another, and so on, until you find a plan which DOES WORK.

"Right here is the point at which the majority of men meet with failure, due to their lack of persistence in creating new plans to take the place of those which fail..."

RULE 3.-PERSIST UNTIL YOU SUCCEED

"I am convinced that about half of what separates the successful entrepreneurs from the non-successful ones is pure perseverance... Unless you have a lot of passion about this, you're not going to survive. You're going to give it up."

Steve Jobs

ACCORDING TO STEVE JOBS bringing a revolutionary project or invention to life is one of the toughest things you can do as an entrepreneur. Not only because it requires hard work but also due to the negative criticism you usually need to confront:

"I've always been attracted to the more revolutionary changes. I don't know why. Because they're harder. They're much more stressful emotionally. And you usually go through a period where everybody tells you that you've completely failed."

Life was not always easy for Jobs. He dropped out of college after realizing that his adoptive parents couldn't handle the financial burden of his education. However, he continued attending classes, including the calligraphy class that years later served as inspiration for the Mac's revolutionary font design and typefaces

Jobs often chased *"impossible dreams"*. Even his co-workers often felt that he would never achieve what they considered his many *"unrealizable goals."* But he proved them wrong.

Similarly, Elon Musk, the multimillionaire co-founder of PayPal and CEO of Tesla and SpaceX, recommends adopting Henry Ford's attitude:

"When Henry Ford made cheap, reliable cars people said, 'Nah, what's wrong with a horse?' That was a huge bet he made, and it worked."

In spite of his humble background, Ford dreamed with producing a *"horseless carriage"* for the masses, and worked on it with for years. Most people said he was crazy.

And, when people finally saw his first automobile crossing the streets of Detroit, many scoffed scornfully. They claimed that his strange machine was not practical and would never be popular. Others claimed that no one in his right mind would ever pay for his machine.

But Ford calmly replied, "*I will belt the earth with dependable motor cars.*" And he did! Thanks to his exceptional dedication and persistence, he not only turned his dream into reality, but he also sold build more vehicles than no other manufacturer.

Years later, when Ford conceived his new V-8 motor, even his engineers said it was impossible.

Nevertheless, paying no attention to their adverse reactions, he planned to build the engine by casting its eight in a single block, which had never been done before.

After telling his engineers to work on the project, they came up with a blueprint of the new engine. However, they warned him that although the project looked good on paper, casting an eight cylinder gas engine block in one piece was absolutely impossible.

"Do it anyway!" Ford exclaimed.

"It's simply not possible!" they objected.

"I don't care! Just do it!" Ford ordered. "Keep working!"

The team got back to work. Of course, they had no choice. It was either following his orders or having to leave the Ford staff for good.

A year passed without results.

They told Ford that they had tried everything conceivable and that there was no way they could ever build such an engine. It was simply *"impossible."*

"Keep trying! Ford insisted.

His engineers kept working and, after analyzing their many failures, the engineers finally managed to learn more about the manufacturing process they sought, until the "impossible" eight cylinder gas engine was born. Ford's determination had won!

WARRIORS OF SUCCESS

Ford is only one of many examples of what an entrepreneur with determination can accomplish. Many successful entrepreneurs, as we shall see, have also proved that in order to succeed, we must first realize that *"each failure brings us a step closer to success."*

CRISIS OFTEN LEADS TO SUCCESS.

In *"Think and Grow Rich,"* Hill states that countless successful people have had a bad start in life. As he sagaciously expresses in his revealing book:

"The turning point in the lives of people who meet success generally arises at the outburst of a crisis in which they are introduced to their 'other selves.'

"Milton was blind, Beethoven was deaf, but they will always be remembered for their success as long as time

endures because they dreamed and translated their dreams into organized thought."

.

CHAPTER HIGHLIGHT

***RULE 3:* PERSIST UNTIL YOU SUCCEED**

Always remember that the turning point in the lives of people who meet success generally arises at the outburst of a crisis in which they are introduced to their 'other selves.' Steve Jobs said one of the toughest things is bringing a revolutionary project or invention to life. It takes persistence to succeed.

The Ten Golden Rules of Entrepreneurial Success

RULE 4.-YOU ARE THE FORGER OF YOUR DESTINY

"Happiness is a state of mind. It's just according to the way you look at things."

Walt Disney

OVER FIVE CENTURIES AGO, William Shakespeare said *"it is not in the stars to hold our destiny but in ourselves."* Unfortunately, countless people still think success and failure are a matter on luck, fate, destiny or some inexplicable force over which we have no control. Unfortunately, they ignore that we are the forgers of our own fortune and misfortune.

Most people, when facing failure, tend to surrender. This explains why countless entrepreneurs who have unsuccessfully pursued financial freedom seek "secure" jobs and become lifelong employees.

Others, driven by negative thinking, never even dare to consider the possibility of becoming entrepreneurs in the first place. Not if they have to leave their secure job. And, although they may even admire entrepreneurs like Jobs or Gates, and silently long for financial freedom, their own fears prevent them from seriously considering it.

HOW WALT DISNEY FACED FAILURE

At age 22, the young American writer Walt Disney was fired from a Missouri newspaper for "*not being creative enough.*" And when he created his first animation company, *Laugh-o-gram Studios*, it sdoon met bankruptcy.

In 1926 he seemingly got lucky. That year, Disney created his first successful animated series, known as *Oswald the Rabbit*, which he sold to Universal Studios. But after he quit working there and tried to continue producing *Oswald* independently, he was sued under the claim that he had no rights to his series. Unfortunately, he had unknowingly ceded the rights of his first successful character when he first signed their contract. And thus, Universal kept the rights of *Oswald the Rabbit*.

In spite of this initial *"failure"* Disney persevered and continued chasing his dreams. And, as w all know, he ultimately met worldwide fame due to his unparalleled creativity and successful animations, being nominated for 59 Academy Awards and winning 32.

As Disney confessed:

"If you can dream it, you can do it... All our dreams can come true if we dare to pursue them."

This fact was wittily summarized by the self-made millionaire Henry Ford, the world's richest man of his time, who warned:

"*Whether you think you* can, or *you* think *you* cannot, *you're* right."

He was right. If you think you will fail, then you most probably will. And that's a lesson we need to keep in mind, for our own thoughts indeed determine our grade of failure or success.

MAKING A HEAVEN OUT OF HELL

As stated four-hundred years ago by the English poet John Milton (1608-1674), failure is only a state of mind.

When Milton was 44 and was barely starting to succeed as a writer he tragically lost his sight. And, to make things worse, scarcely three months after going blind, his wife died, and their one-year-old son soon followed. He was completely shattered!

Not only was he affected by his unexpected visual impairment, but another type of obscurity suddenly fell upon him: the gloom of endless blackness and growing despair. Many have gone mad or killed themselves for less. But not Milton.

Driven by a lifelong quest for higher understanding and great persistence, Milton resisted to what many would agree to call a *"Hell on Earth."*

Instead of quitting, he learned from his mistakes and adopted a new attitude, he managed to *"see"* a half-filled cup instead of a half empty one, thus turning darkness into light.

During the years that followed his tragedy, Milton not only remarried and fathered more children, but he also hired a secretary, resumed his writing career and dictated his literary masterpiece, *"Lost Paradise"*...

In spite of his blindness, Milton literally *"made a Heaven out of Hell"*:

> **"The mind is its own place**
> **and in itself can make**
> **a Heaven of Hell,**
> **a Hell of Heaven."**

Referring to his loss of sight, he said in his *"Lost Paradise"*:

> **"To be blind is not miserable;**
> **What is miserable is**
> **not being able to bear blindness."**

Milton found that the real source of failure consists in *"making a Hell out of Heaven"* and continuously filling our heads with endless negative thoughts.

Regrettably, instead of a source of profound lessons, many see failure as something absolutely catastrophic, thus committing a huge mistake.

Like I said, you are the forger of your own destiny. And unless you realize it, your own fears will prevent you from reaching your most cherished goals.

CHAPTER HIGHLIGHT

***RULE 4:* YOU ARE THE FORGER OF YOUR DESTINY**

Over five centuries ago, William Shakespeare noted that "it is not in the stars to hold our destiny but in ourselves." Don't be like countless entrepreneurs who fail only to turn to "secure" jobs and become lifelong employees or like those driven by negative thinking who never even dare to consider the possibility of becoming entrepreneurs in the first place. You are the forger of your own destiny. And unless you realize it, your own fears will prevent you from reaching your most cherished goals.

RULE 5.- GRASP THE POWER OF THE UNCONSCIOUS

"Properly speaking, the unconscious is the real psychic; its inner nature is just as unknown to us as the reality of the external world, and it is just as imperfectly reported to us through the data of consciousness as is the external world through the indications of our sensory organs..."

Sigmund Freud

NAPOLEON HILL CAME TO THIS WORLD in a humble log cabin in Wise County, Virginia, on October 1883. Although is parents were poor, he had the good fortune of growing up in a loving family and become dully educated.

His was a time of significant change and transformation never before experienced by humankind.

As he openly admitted in the Preface of the last book that he wrote, "*Grow Rich With Peace of Mind*", published at the age of eighty-four (scarcely a couple of years before his death in 1970), during his long and productive life he had the chance to witness more "vital changes in the affairs of men" than those produced bfor his lifetime:

"*I have seen the advent of the automobile, the airplane, radio, television, atomic power, the age of space.*

"*I have seen electric power spread across the country, industry rise to levels of production beyond nineteenth-century dreams, science and technology enjoy an almost explosive development...*

Although he did not mention it, Hill also witnessed another revolutionary breakthrough:

The first scientific studies of the unconscious and the official birth of psychoanalysis.

FREUD AND THE UNCONSCIOUS

The first scientist to methodically study and elaborate a psychological theory of the unconscious was the Viennese neurologist Sigmund Freud, also known as the Father of Psychoanalysis.

Freud based his revolutionary theory on the fact that the human mind operates in two basic stages or layers: A superficial one, known as the *"conscious,"* and a deep one, hidden in our minds, known as the *"unconscious."*

He defined the unconscious as *"a special psychic realm with wish-impulses of its own, with its own method of expression and with a psychic mechanism peculiar to itself, all of which ordinarily are not in force."*

This dual nature of the human mind is the basis of what is known as the *"iceberg model."* It compares the mind with a huge iceberg, stating that our conscious mind is only *"the tip of the iceberg"* and that our enormous and unseen unconscious hides deep beneath the surface.

Just like a floating iceberg (or an ice cube, for that matter) the mind mostly sinks into the water, with only a small part surfacing, which represents our "conscious mind", which only represents a small percentage of the whole human mental apparatus.

Freud was the first scientist to determine that the workings of our thinking mind mostly take place in the deep and hidden layers of the unconscious – totally without our conscious awareness.

Freud was also the first to compare the unconscious with a vast *"storage-room"* (memory drive or hard disk) where all the information or data we have gathered since birth is kept and processed, including all our unconscious thinking patterns and repetitive reactions.

According to him, our unconscious runs and controls our conscious mind, and based on this he defined analytical therapy as the way of inducing mental sanity by *"turning unconscious processes into conscious awareness."*

CREATIVITY AND THE UNCONSCIOUS

One of the advantages of getting to know your unconscious and establishing a relationship with it is that you can learn how to unleash your creativity.

All our creative ideas come from our unconscious. And none of the world's greatest entrepreneurs would have succeeded had they not been creative.

The German physicist Albert Einstein (1879-1955), also known as the Father of Relativity, stated that *"imagination is more important than knowledge."* And he was right.

He also admitted:

"When I examine myself and my methods of thought," he confessed, *"I come to the conclusion that, than my talent for absorbing positive knowledge, the gift of fantasy has meant more to me ... Imagination is more important than knowledge. Knowledge is limited. Imagination encircles the world..."*

And Napoleon Hill wrote:

"All achievements, all earned riches, have their beginning in an idea." Although there are countless

definitions of creativity, let's see what Steve Jobs wrote on the subject:

"Creativity is just connecting things. When you ask creative people how they did something, they feel a little guilty because they didn't really do it, they just saw something.

Remember this:

"Creativity is just connecting things".

To fully understand creativity and its hidden process, in the late 1980s the University of California psychologist Dean Keith Simonton studied the career trajectories of hundreds of eminent creative people and concluded that "creative genius" depends on the ability to combine (connect) random and unrelated ideas in new and useful ways.

This combinatory process is mostly done in an unconscious level and is the basis of his "Theory of Scientific Genius", presented in his book Scientific Genius: A Psychology Of Science (1988), and later expanded in Origins of Genius: Darwinian Perspectives on Creativity (1999) and Creativity in Science: Chance, Logic, Genius, and Zeitgeist (2004).

Simonton claims that "geniuses are geniuses" because they are able to form "more combinations than the merely talented individuals" plus they also recognize the most innovative and useful combinations, trashing the rest.

According to Simonton:

"Creativity is the ability of forming innovative and useful combinations of pre-existing ideas or elements."

CREATIVE IDEAS AND INSPIRATION

Creative ideas have been defined in many ways throughout history, from sparks of inspirations sent by the gods or muses, to conscious insights produced by the hidden mechanisms of the unconscious.

Based on Simonton's theory, we will use the following definition:

"A creative idea is the result of an innovative and useful combination of pre-existing concepts and ideas."

The first man of science to mention that new ideas depend on pre-existing elements was the French philosopher and mathematician René Descartes (1596-1650), who in his *Meditations on First Philosophy* stated:

"When painters desire to represent sirens and little satyrs with utterly unfamiliar shapes, they cannot devise altogether new natures for them, but simply combine parts from different animals; or if perhaps they do think up something so new that nothing at all like it has ever been seen, which is thus altogether fictitious and false, it is certain that at least the colors which they combine to form images must be real.."

Let´s take a look at a few examples:

When Leonardo da Vinci, for instance, designed the world´s first flying machines he studied the flight of birds and combined these facts with his knowledge of mechanics, transforming his pre-existing ideas into new ones.

Gutenberg, on the other hand, invented the printing press by combining the ideas of the wine press and the coin punch.

The first automobiles were also the result of combining pre-existing ideas, in this case by combining a four-wheeled carriage with a combustion engine.

Edison invented the light bulb by combining the principles of electrical conductivity and vacuum incandescence.

And Einstein created his famous equation, E=mc2 by simply combining three pre-existing concepts: energy, mass, and speed of light. By simply combining or connecting these three concepts, he literally transformed the way we perceive the universe.

And this brings us back to what Steve Jobs said:

"*Creativity is just connecting things.*"

.

CHAPTER HIGHLIGHT

***RULE 5:* UNDERSTAND THE POWER OF THE UNCONSCIOUS**

According to the psychological theory of the Viennese neurologist Sigmund Freud, also known as the Father of Psychoanalysis, the mind has two basic layers: A superficial one, known as the "conscious," and a deep one, hidden in our deepest minds, known as the "unconscious," considered as "a special psychic realm with wish-impulses of its own". According to him, our unconscious runs and controls our conscious mind. With the right attitude, we can benefit from our unconscious and its endless creative potential.

RULE 6.- OBSERVE YOUR THINKING PATTERNS

"The human brain is an incredible pattern-matching machine."

Jeff Bezos

ACCORDING TO SCIENTIFIC RESEARCH, most humans have between sixty and one thousand different thoughts each day. And about 90% of these are repetitive, pre-programmed thoughts that determine how we behave and react on a daily basis.

As we shall see, digesting this truth is the golden gateway that leads to positivity and success.

One of the first modern psychologists to stress the importance of thoughts and how these actually influence our perception of reality was the nineteenth-century researcher and philosopher William James (1842-1910) who over a century ago noted:

"Man can alter his life by altering his thinking... While part of what we perceive comes through our senses from the objects around us, another part (perhaps the larger) always comes from our own head."

This same truth was also expressed almost two thousand years ago by the Roman emperor and philosopher Marcus Aurelius Antoninus (121-180 AD), who expressed the following in his celebrated *"Meditations"*:

"Our life is what our thoughts make it... If you are distressed by something external, the pain is not due to

the thing itself but to your own opinion about it, and thus you have the power to revoke it at any moment... All we hear is just an opinion, not a fact. All we see is a perspective, not the real truth."

POSITIVE VS. NEGATIVE VIEWS OF REALITY

Whenever we fail or come face to face with a seemingly unavoidable or threatening obstacle, we are momentarily invaded by fear and negative thoughts. But, whether we sink deep into negativity or snap out of it will strictly depend on us.

If most of our recurrent thoughts are negative, then our overall view of life will become negative, distorting our perception of reality to the point of producing a 'mirage' or 'illusion' that only exists in our own minds.

Almost two thousand years ago, after studying how our mind works and its effect on our personal view f things, the celebrated Greek philosopher Epictetus (55-135 AD) concluded:

"People are not disturbed by things, but by the view they take of these."

As mentioned, if most of our recurring thoughts directly affect our overall view of life, distorting our perception of reality to the point of producing a 'mirage' or 'illusion' that only exists in our own minds. This explains why some of us always see a half-empty cup while others see it half-full.

The cause and influence of these psychological 'mirages' or 'illusions' were first studied in the 1960s by the American psychiatrist and University of Pennsylvania professor Aaron T. Beck, also known as the Father of Cognitive Therapy, who decided to call them "*cognitive distortions.*"

Defined as altered perceptions of reality, Beck concluded that these "*cognitive distortions*" are produced and sustained by our repetitive self-talk and that, in the case of depressed or stressed individuals, they are caused by the regular repetition of negative thoughts, such as:

"*I am a failure*"

"*I cannot do anything right!*"

"*I am so clumsy!*"

We all have our own versions of these or similar repetitive negative affirmations. They seem to pop in our heads involuntarily each time things turn out wrong. However, while some people can discard them as soon as they appear others usually get stuck.

What about you? What do you usually repeat to yourself each time you fail or feel stressed out? In these cases, do you mostly have negative or primarily positive thoughts?

TWO SIDES OF THE COIN

To illustrate the effects of our *"cognitive distortions"* and how this powerful psychological phenomenon is boosted by our repetitive thinking patterns, in my book "Stop negative thinking... etc."

Let's look at the hypothetical case of two young graduates, fresh out of business school, who happen to be identical twins: the Smith brothers Bill and Joe. Suppose they both have a job interview in an important company.

Apart from looking almost exactly alike they share similar physical and mental conditions and potentials.

They were both raised in the same family, attended the same school and, at first glance, nobody can tell them apart. However, there is a huge difference in the way they think.

Let's start out with Joe. He is a pessimistic young man who generally repeats negative thoughts to himself, such as:

"I hate myself"

"No one likes me"

"I'm a failure"

"I will never succeed"

"I'm a loser"

"I feel so sad"

His brother Bill, on the other hand, in times of trouble generally repeats to himself positive or optimistic affirmations like:

"Don't worry, be happy"

"No pain no gain"

"I love myself"

"Life is beautiful"

"I'm a winner"

"I feel so good"

And so, while Bill always sees a half-full glass, Joe always sees it half-empty.

Fact is, Bill sees a world of opportunities and success, whereas Joe only sees a world of failure and sadness.

Who do you think is more likely to get the job and succeed in life?

A DIFFERENT WORLD IN EACH HEAD

As we saw, the twin brothers I mentioned earlier seem to live in two different worlds. They evidently hold dissimilar perceptions of reality and of themselves.

Due to Joe's negative thinking, he sees himself as a potential failure, unable to reach success, while Bill perceives himself as a successful person willing to face problems and work his way to success.

They each have different mental perceptions of themselves, based on their own personal ideas and beliefs: As we have seen, while one is evidently optimistic, the second is seemingly pessimistic.

Joe, who is possessed by his own repetitive negative thinking, represents the state of mind maintained by most people in the world, who unconsciously repeat negative thoughts to themselves without ever realizing it.

Joe´s perception of himself undoubtedly affects him, creating self-inflicted tension, insecurity, sadness, fear, rage, suffering, and depression, among other consequences. What´s his biggest mistake?

Not being able to realize that his personal perception of the world and of himself are only the product of his own imagination!

He's got the same potential and chances of succeeding as his twin brother. He has all he needs to succeed. But due to his constant negative thinking, he cannot realize it.

Regrettably, most of us are just like Joe.

Influenced by our repetitive negative thinking, we too have created a false perception of the world and of ourselves.

In sum, as the German-American spiritual coach Eckhart Tolle claims:

"Almost every human body is under a great deal of strain and stress, not because some external factor threatens it but from within the mind."

OPTIMISM AND SCIENTIFIC RESEARCH

Optimism is a state of mind characterized by positive thoughts and the constant and motivating belief that our plans and goals are easily achievable, and that with due effort we can overcome all obstacles. It is "the psychological resource that enables us to cope with adverse situations."

Optimism can improve our psychological and physical wellbeing, and can also help us avoid and recover from illness. It seems to have a meaningful impact on the perceived quality of life of ill people due to the fact that it enhances our capability of coping with tension and stress.

The good news is that you can learn to be an optimist by changing the perception of the world around you. This is why it is said that *"when you change the way you see things, the things you see change."*

The fact that optimists and pessimists cope differently with problems has been studied for decades.

One of these studies took a group of undergraduates and asked them to recall the single most stressful event they had faced during the preceding month. While optimists focused on solutions and the fact that stressful events can be controlled, pessimists focused on their problems and on the difficulties of maintaining their goals when facing stressful situations.

While optimists tended to accept the reality of stressful events, pessimists tended to rely on such tactics as denial and substance abuse to evade reality and lessen their awareness of the problems at hand. Also, optimism can confer psychological and physical benefits, including the reduction of stress.

Based on the above, it is plain to see why optimistic entrepreneurs always maintain a positive perspective and love their work. They simply know that, with the required effort, they will be able to meet their goals no matter what.

CHAPTER HIGHLIGHT

***RULE 6:* OBSERVE YOUR THINKING PATTERNS**

According to scientific research, most humans have between sixty and one thousand different thoughts each day. And about 90% of these are repetitive, pre-programmed thoughts that determine how we behave and react on a daily basis. Only by identifying our negative thinking patterns and voluntarily changing these for positive ones, we can become optimists and therefore begin to transit the golden gateway that leads to success.

RULE 7.- MAKE YOUR AFFIRMATIONS A HABIT

"Every thought entirely filling our mind becomes true for us and tends to transform itself into action."

Emile Coué

ALTHOUGH SIGMUND FREUD is universally remembered as the Father of Psychoanalysis, he was not the first scientist to methodically study the role of the unconscious and how our repetitive-thought patterns alter our general perception of the world and ourselves.

In fact, several decades before Freud published his first works, pioneer studies were conducted in Europe, mainly in France, where several renowned psychologists investigated this matter as early as 1866.

In 1910, the French psychologist and pharmacist Émile Coué de la Châtaigneraie (1857-1926) introduced a popular method of psychotherapy and self-improvement based on what he called *"optimistic autosuggestion."*

After opening a clinic in Nancy, France, he attended thousands of patients over the next sixteen years using the method of conscious autosuggestion, consisting in the repetition of mantra-like affirmations to improve health.

According to his theory, the repetition of words and mental images enough times can cause significant changes in the subconscious. One of his most popular treatments consisted of telling his patients to repeat the following positive affirmation at least twenty times when starting and ending each day:

"Day by day, in every way, I am getting better and better."

Although Coué's theories were most popular in Europe, they also spread in America and became famous in their own right thanks to the works of Norman Vincent Peale, Maxwell Maltz, Robert H. Schuller, W. Napoleon Hill, and Clement Stone.

Coué realized that it is far better to focus on and imagine the desired, positive results. He recognized the value of traditional medicine. But he also acknowledged that negative thought patterns always affect our health. His treatment was based on repetition of a positive affirmation with the object of replacing his patient's *"illness thoughts"* with *"healing thoughts,"* allowing them to actually cure themselves quicker and more efficiently.

REPETITION AND AUTOSUGGESTION

Coué was the first scientist to determine that the use of constant affirmations is a two-way street that can be both beneficial as well as harmful, declaring that:

"It can wound or even kill you if you handle it imprudently and unconsciously. Contrarily, it can even save your life if you know how to us it consciously."

For example, negative thoughts like *"I don't feel well"* or *"I'm sick"* can act as autosuggestions and encourage our mind and body to accept these facts and actually deteriorate our health.

Stressing the importance of keeping this fact in mind, Coué stated that:

"Autosuggestion is a tool that we are born with, and with which we unconsciously play all our life, as a baby plays with his rattle."

Napoleon Hill both studied and practiced Coue's methods. In *"Think and Grow Rich"* he not only acknowledges the effectiveness of Coué's methods but he also explained them:

"Nature has so built man that he has absolute control over that which reaches his subconscious mind... but this does not mean that that man always exercises this

control. He does not, in most cases, which explains why so many go through life in poverty."

A FAMOUS FORMULA

In 1922, Emile Coué published the first English edition of his revealing book "*Self Mastery Through Conscious Autosuggestion,*" in which he wrote:

"Before sending off your patient, you must tell him that he carries within him the instrument that can cure him, and that you can teach him how to use it...

"Thus, every morning before rising, and every night on getting into bed, he must shut his eyes and in thought transport himself into your presence, and then repeat twenty times consecutively in a monotonous voice, counting using a string with twenty knots in it, this little phrase:

"EVERY DAY, IN EVERY RESPECT, I AM GETTING BETTER AND BETTER."

According to Hill, the mere repetition of these words is useless unless you mix emotion and faith with them:

"You will not get appreciable results until you learn to reach your subconscious mind with thoughts, or spoken words which have been well emotionalized with belief.

THE DIRECTING POWER OF AFFIRMATIONS

It is said that confidence impels achievement, for it focuses on our abilities, mental faculties and inner power.

You'll find a wonderful advantage if you start out every morning with positive affirmations and thoughts of prosperity. This will let you view your problems from a different perspective and will serve as a powerful tonic for your physical and mental health.

Do not let unhappy or discordant thoughts in your mind. Instead of this, replace these thoughts with cheerful and optimistic affirmations and you'll quickly modify your negative thinking patterns.

Constant affirmations increases courage, and courage is the backbone of confidence.

Boosting your confidence, however, is only possible with a positive state of mind -never with a negative one.

Most people, unfortunately, are always influenced by the opinions of others and cannot hold positive ideas about themselves on their own, ignoring that unless true conviction takes hold of them, they will experience scarce achievements in life.

Why? Because if your thoughts are weak, then you will also be weak and your work futile. On the other hand, if you use the power of positive affirmations, that is, if you affirm that you can succeed, then you will most probably succeed, overcoming all difficulties, obstacles, and misfortunes.

Napoleon Hill first highlighted the relationship between positive affirmations and the achievement of life goals in his 1925 publication *"The Law of Success in 16 Lessons"*, a multi-volume correspondence course containing what he called *"a success formula for the average person."*

After examining more than 16,000 men and women, he concluded the following:

*Ninety-five percent of the people he examined were clear "failures". They held jobs they did not like and *had no chief goal in life.*

*Only five percent were clear "successes." This minority , while worked on what they loved best and had definite *purposes and plans* in life.

TAKING CONTROL OF YOUR AFFIRMATIONS

As the author and publishing entrepreneur Louise Hay expressed, *"affirmations are statements that reinforce a positive or negative belief.*

By observing your thoughts, you will soon be able to identify your most common negative-thinking patterns and thus create positive affirmations to counteract these.

It is important to spend five minutes three times per day reciting your affirmations. You should write them down and post them in places where you will see them all day such as your mirror.

SAMPLES OF POSITIVE AFFIRMATIONS:

• Each day brings in new opportunities

• I deserve to have financial abundance in my life NOW.

• I AM successful because I know what I want and I ask for it.

• I define success my way and each day I create it.

• I have a wonderful job and give wonderful service for wonderful pay.

- My prosperity is unlimited. My success is unlimited.

- My business path is always perfect for me.

- Abundance and I are one.

- I HAVE unlimited abundance.

- Abundance surrounds me. Today I claim my share.

CHAPTER HIGHLIGHT

***RULE 7:* MAKE YOUR AFFIRMATIONS A HABIT**

A popular practice that allows you to replace negative thinking patterns with positive ones, consists in repeating affirmations such as "Day by day, in every way, I am getting better and better." Do this at least twenty times when rising and going to bed. And avoid repeating negative thoughts, for these can encourage our mind and body to accept these facts and affect us negatively.

RULE 8.- ESCAPE FROM NEGATIVE THINKING

"*A negative mental attitude is one of the primary causes of failure.*"

Napoleon Hill

A. J. P A R R

NEGATIVE THINKING PATTERNS constitute the primordial difference between failure and success, happiness and unhappiness, scarcity and wealth. So, we should elude them.

These patterns always increase our pessimism and tell us to desist, to give up, to stop hoping, crowding out our positive thoughts and building up negative emotions. And, as experience shows, this stored negativity is always toxic and generates even more negative thoughts.

Negative thoughts are known to increase the production of negative feelings, including grief, anxiety, irritation, and despair. They are produced automatically and to us they appear to be reasonable and believable.

The act of thinking repeatedly about past events is known as rumination. We engage in this type of thinking when trying to make sense of our problems and why they happened, thinking that this will somehow help us reach a better understanding of our problems and make us better. However, dwelling on the past and focusing on why bad things have happened cannot always help. Being stuck in the past actually maintains depression and is unhelpful.

Instead of dwelling on the past, we better ask ourselves how we can make things any better.

The following are some questions you can ask yourself to help challenge unhelpful thinking. It can be good idea to write down your answers so that you can read them when needed.

1). Is it helpful to think in this way? - If not, Why not?

2). If I continue to thinking and acting this way, will I feel better or worse?

3). What would you say to a friend who was being so critical of him/herself? - Would you agree with them? - If not, why not?

CHAPTER HIGHLIGHT

RULE 8: ESCAPE FROM NEGATIVE THINKINGO

Negative thinking patterns constitute the primordial difference between failure and success, happiness and unhappiness, scarcity and wealth. To protect yourself against negative influences, whether of your own making or the result of the activities of negative people around you, you must concentrate on positive thoughts and affirmations, for "the mind can produce anything it can conceive and believe".

RULE 9.-DISCOVER THE POWER OF MEDITATION

"With the 'Seinfeld', I was doing a TV series in which I was the star of the show, the executive producer of the show, the head writer, in charge of casting and editing, for 24 episodes on network television—not cable—for nine years! And I'm just a normal guy. And that was not a normal situation to be in... So I meditated every day. And that's how I survived the nine years."

Jerry Seinfeld

TWO OF THE UNWANTED CONSEQUENCES of working hard are stress and anxiety. If you suffer from these or wish to avoid them, I recommend practicing mini-meditations.

Only a few minutes will suffice.

Do not worry if you don´t have time to engage yourself in a lengthy daily meditation practice. There is no need to. ***Just practice several mini-meditations during the day, or whenever you feel too anxious or stressed.***

According to scientific research, several minutes per day of meditation practice brings calmness and provides increasing levels of wellbeing and inner peace, allowing us to view life from a new perspective and solve our daily problems in creative new ways.

A revealing Mayo Clinic report states that effectively "meditation can wipe away the day's stress, bringing with it inner peace… If stress has you anxious, tense and worried, consider trying meditation. Spending even a few minutes in meditation can restore your calm and inner peace… Meditation can bring you a sense of peace and calmness, boosting your emotional well-being and your overall health. It can help carry you more calmly through your day and may improve certain medical conditions..."

The Mayo Clinic report mentions the following "emotional benefits of meditation":

Gaining a new perspective on stressful situations

Building skills to manage your stress

Increasing self-awareness

Focusing on the present

Reducing negative emotions

The same report also states that meditation may improve certain medical conditions "especially those that may be worsened by stress", such as:

Anxiety disorders

Asthma

Cancer

Depression

Heart disease

High blood pressure

*Pain

*Sleep problems

According to an independent study published in 2012 on the effects of meditation on the process of "aging", scientists at the University of California at Los Angeles and Nobel Prize winner Elizabeth Blackburn found that 12 minutes of daily yoga meditation for eight weeks increased an improvement of up to 43 percent in "stress-induced aging". Blackburn of the University of California, San Francisco, shared the Nobel medicine prize in 2009 with Carol Greider and Jack Szostak for research on the "immortality enzyme" (telomerase) known to slow the "cellular aging" process.

THE RULER OF YOUR MIND

Most people believe they control their minds. But most people are wrong. We are constantly having thoughts that are beyond our direct control. And these thoughts are the product of involuntary processes based on "automatic psychological responses or reactions" produced unconsciously, that is, involuntarily and therefore beyond our conscious control.

BREATH MEDITATION PRACTICE

The following practice, known as breath meditation, can calm you chattering mind and let you experience the "here and now". A few minutes per session (even one or two) will do.

To practice it anytime and anywhere you need, just follow these simple steps:

STEP 1:

Sit or lie down in a comfortable and relaxing position and close your eyes. Any position will do.

STEP 2:

Take a deep breath. A single, conscious breath can calm your mind where there was only an uninterrupted succession of thought after thought.

STEP 3:

Concentrate on the sound of your breath. Listen to it as the air enters and leaves your lungs. Feel it. Do not try to control it.

If a thought arises, do not engage yourself in an inner conversation with yourself. Simply, be aware of your thought and release it, letting it go without second thoughts.

Recognize that by focusing on your breath you are experiencing the "here and now". Forget the future and the past, at least for now, and concentrate on the present moment.

STEP 4:

Keep focusing on your breath and the silence that exists between each inspiration and expiration. As you listen, also "feel" the movement of your lungs, the movement of your chest and abdomen slowly expanding and contracting as the air moves in and out... Don´t try to control your breath. Let it be. Feel it. Experience it.

STEP 5:

As you continue breathing, realize that breathing isn't something you do but something you witness or observe.

STEP 6:

Repeat this several times per day, FOR AT LEAST ONE OR TWO MINUTES AT A TIME. Don´t judge your thoughts or start an inner chat. Just focus on your breath and experience the "here and now", without second thoughts.

You can repeat this exercise in "stressful situations", when it is imperative to keep calm instead of losing yourself in your own thoughts and worries.

You can practice when driving to or from work, walking, waiting for someone, or whenever you find yourself in any of the following situations:

*Excessively "tied up" in your own thoughts and can't stop thinking.

*Excessively stressed

*Excessively worried

*Excessively angry

*Excessively sad

*Excessively excited

*Excessively confused

*Excessively afraid

*Excessively insomniac.

*Excessively discouraged.

*Excessively depressed.

*Excessively nervous.

In sum, starting today you can use this technique to actually help you ANY TIME YOU NEED TO STOP THINKING NEGATIVELY, anywhere and anytime, including when you are:

*Walking

*Driving

*Going up or down stairs.

*In the elevator.

*In the bus, subway or cab.

*Waiting in line.

*Waiting for someone.

*Taking a short break at work.

*Eating.

*Taking a bath.

*Going to the bathroom.

*Having sex.

*Doing your daily activities.

.

CHAPTER HIGHLIGHTS

RULE 9: DISCOVER THE POWER OF MEDITATION

According to scientific research, meditation can bring you a sense of peace and calmness, boosting your emotional well-being and your overall health. It can help carry you more calmly through your day and may improve certain medical conditions.

Its practice provides increasing levels of wellbeing and inner peace, allowing us to view life from a new perspective and solve our daily problems in creative new ways.

Breath meditation can calm you chattering mind in only a few minutes (at least one or two will do).

RULE 10.-DEVELOP A WINNING MINDSET

"*Failure is not the opposite of success; it's part of success... Take risks. Failure is a stepping stone to success.*"

Arianna Huffington

MOST TOP "*BUSINESS GURUS*" SUGGEST that we have the power to decide how we react to specific situations, and control these reactions. All it take is the right training. Above all, developing a winning mindset and adopting a positive mental attitude is a crucial factor in determining whether or not move forward in our entrepreneurial life.

Knowing what you want and going for it with the right mindset will allow you to focus on what is working well in your life, your strengths and those of others, and the lessons derived from all your experiences, whether good or bad, empowering or crushing. It is a matter of focusing on what truly matters.

The case of the multimillionaire entrepreneur Arianna Huffington is also worth observing. After a rough divorce, back when she was neither rich nor famous, she decided to run for Governor of California, precisely against Arnold Schwarzenegger.

Of course, Arianna lost. But, instead of sinking in despair, she "reinvented" herself and, using the web's growing popularity, she started her own website and planted the seed of what came to be known as The HuffPost. But her new venture had a rough start. It not only faced a steep financial crisis but was also accused of promoting false beliefs and plagiarism. Even though many of her colleagues predicted her rotund failure, Huffington persevered against all odds and eventually turned her site into one of the most successful news media of all times.

In 2009, she **was named as number 12 in Forbe's** first-ever list of the Most Influential Women In Media. She later sold her online business for over $300 million to AOL. And in 2014 Forbes named her as the 52nd Most Powerful Woman in the World.

According to her, tu succeed we must first understand the role of failure:

"Failure is not the opposite of success; it's part of success... Take risks. Failure is a stepping stone to success."

So, if you're feeling stuck in a rut and want to build a winning mindset, try the following tips and give yourself a head start in terms of improving your present mindset and achieving your entrepreneurial goals starting today:

1.-AVOID NEGATIVE INFLUENCES

Negative influences work on you through your subconscious mind and are therefore difficult to detect. To avoid these, deliberately seek the company of positive people and stay away from negative ones, for these are always damaging. Positive influences, on the contrary, are always beneficial.

Optimistic thoughts are always focused on positive and productive activities such as work, errands, studies and enjoyable events. They focus on the present moment, not on the future or past. They focus on their loved ones, friends, pets and things that that make them happy; on positive and productive endeavors and activities here and now, including work, hobbies, errands, celebrations, vacations, etc. They are not thoughts about "what if" scenarios and future possibilities. They are not thoughts about revenge or getting even.

2.-RECOGNIZE YOUR NEGATIVE THOUGHTS

Negative thoughts are ego-oriented thoughts. The ego-oriented thoughts that are negative are self - oriented thoughts that make you feel unhappy or bad. These include thoughts that judge self or others, thoughts that make you feel like a victim, feel self-pity, feel fear or feel anger or hate. They also include thoughts about controlling, hurting or deceiving others.

In spite of the above, negative thoughts play an essential role in our lives and should not always be suppressed. When they occur, acknowledge them and understand what they are telling you about yourself and others. They often tell you what and who irritates you, what and who to avoid and what you need to deal with. The negative often leads us to the positive. From the negative, you can develop and execute plans to deal with situations and move toward a positive outcome.

To be a positive thinker, you must elevate soul over your ego in governance of self and assert control of your thoughts through application of faith and will. So, make positive people, images and things the objects of your thoughts for your thoughts always determine your emotional state.

3.- AVOID NEGATIVE SELF-TALK

Your inner voice or self-talk is one of the most important aspects in your quest to become the most positive you can be. Be aware of your inner voice and what it says to you.

Positive self-talk is making what you say to yourself on a daily basis as optimistic as possible, so that you can favorably influence your emotions, outlook and actions. Positive self-talk, if used effectively, can be extremely powerful. It not only can result in you thinking much more positively but can also play a decisive role in your entrepreneurial success.

One way of using it effectively is to be as upbeat as possible when you are engaging in it. This doubles the impact as you are not only hearing positive words, but you are also doing something positive with your body.

With practice, you can train it to say positive, motivating and encouraging things to you. This way, you can start to take control of your thoughts and hence your actions.

Richard Branson, for example, recommends always being confident and concrete when expressing your business plans, avoiding language like "with some luck, we will..." or "we hope that...".

In Neuro-Linguistic Programming (NLP), a branch of personal development that looks at how our minds can be re-programmed such that negative habits are unlearnt, this is called reframing. Reframing means either using different thinking patterns or alternative words to put situations into a different perspective.

A useful exercise is to divide a piece of paper in half and write the negative words you tend to use on the left hand side, and their corresponding, more positive alternatives on the right.

For example you may write "problem" on the left and "challenge" on the right, or "I cannot" on the left and "how can I?" on the right. This simple but powerful exercise will make you more aware of the negative words you habitually use, and how you can change them.

Since Neuro-linguistic programming (NLP) is an active form of psychological therapy, its capability to help us eliminate negative behavior is positively unique as compared with other forms of psychological therapies.

NLP works through restructuring our learned or programmed negative behaviors that affects our way of thinking and communication. In other words, since our mind is trained to learn from what we see, we sometimes see things negatively especially if someone has caused us great pain, embarrassment and failures.

This traumatic feeling causes us phobias, depression, psychosomatic illnesses, bad habits, and depression and learning disorders. Through time if we cannot eliminate these negative feelings they can greatly affect our whole being. This is where NLP works.

NLP can model human behavior and psychotherapists and hypnotherapists use it to eliminate negative behaviors and change it into positive behaviors. Negative behaviors also include habit disorders, psychosomatic problems and learning disabilities.

These debilitating mental disorders can render us mentally incapable of clear thinking, so experts apply direct examples and hands-on experiential training to reprogram our mind with positive thinking and improve our interaction with other people.

The positive effect of NLP is particularly on improving communication, developing self motivation, enhancing memory, building relationships and developing positive behavioral patterns which are all most necessary especially if our career revolves on corporate environment such as in education, human resources, management, sales and marketing, counseling, coaching, and training.

In conclusion, NLP can boost our personal and interpersonal development.

While, in general, we may apply NLP for self motivation and improvement, we can also use it to maximize our power to influence people and live fuller, better lives.

4.- THE KEY OF A WINNING MINDSET

When starting out a new business, a lot of people like to make excuses like "I don't have money or connections. I don't have this or that." But, once you find something that you like to do and turn it into a business, you will stop making excuses. The worst thing that can happen is that you're going to have fun doing what you love to do and also learn from your actions and mistakes. However, in the best case, you can end up turning your passion into a successful business.

Of course, there is more to success and meeting your aspirations than merely following some simple rules found in a book. Just keep in mind that success directly depends on your personal patterns of thought and behavior.

For best results, read this book at least once more, for repetition is vital when adopting new thinking patterns. Especially if you seek to master The Ten Golden *Rules of Entrepreneurial Success and Financial Wealth* detailed in this work:

RULE 1 - **HEED THE LESSONS OF FAILURE**

Perhaps the hardest part for many consists in having to face multiple failures before succeeding. As Sir Richard Branson explains: "If you're an entrepreneur and your first venture wasn't a success, there's no need for the F word (Failure). Learn from it. Pick yourself up. And try; try again."

RULE 2 - **ALWAYS RISE AFTER YOU FALL**

According to Tony Robbins, sometimes the problems we find in life are exactly what we require to become the best version of ourselves. To those who experience failure and do not know what to do, Napoleon Hill recommends immediately working on a new plan, as expressed in "Think and Grow Rich": "If the first plan fails, replace it with a new one."

RULE 3 - **PERSIST UNTIL YOU SUCCEED**

Always remember that the turning point in the lives of people who meet success generally arises at the outburst of a crisis in which they are introduced to their 'other selves.' Steve Jobs said one of the toughest things is bringing a revolutionary project or invention to life. It takes persistence to succeed.

RULE 4 - **YOU ARE THE FORGER OF YOUR DESTINY**

Over five centuries ago, William Shakespeare noted that "it is not in the stars to hold our destiny but in ourselves." Don't be like countless entrepreneurs who fail only to turn to "secure" jobs and become lifelong employees or like those driven by negative thinking who never even dare to consider the possibility of becoming entrepreneurs in the first place. You are the forger of your own destiny. And unless you realize it, your own fears will prevent you from reaching your most cherished goals.

RULE 5 - **UNDERSTAND THE POWER OF THE UNCONSCIOUS**

According to the psychological theory of the Viennese neurologist Sigmund Freud, also known as the Father of Psychoanalysis, the mind has two basic layers: A superficial one, known as the "conscious," and a deep one, hidden in our deepest minds, known as the "unconscious," considered as "a special psychic realm with wish-impulses of its own".

According to him, our unconscious runs and controls our conscious mind. With the right attitude, we can benefit from our unconscious and its endless creative potential.

RULE 6 - **OBSERVE YOUR THINKING PATTERNS**

According to scientific research, most humans have between sixty and one thousand different thoughts each day. And about 90% of these are repetitive, pre-programmed thoughts that determine how we behave and react on a daily basis. Only by identifying our negative thinking patterns and voluntarily changing these for positive ones, we can become optimists and therefore begin to transit the golden gateway that leads to success.

RULE 7 - MAKE YOUR AFFIRMATIONS A HABIT

A popular practice that allows you to replace negative thinking patterns with positive ones, consists in repeating affirmations such as "Day by day, in every way, I am getting better and better." Do this at least twenty times when starting and ending each day. Repeating negative thoughts can encourage our mind and body to accept these facts and actually affect you negatively.

RULE 8 - ESCAPE FROM NEGATIVE THINKING

Negative thinking patterns constitute the primordial difference between failure and success, happiness and unhappiness, scarcity and wealth. To protect yourself against negative influences, whether of your own making or the result of the activities of negative people around you, you must concentrate on positive thoughts and affirmations, for "the mind can produce anything it can conceive and believe".

RULE 9 - DISCOVER THE POWER OF MEDITATION

According to scientific research, meditation can bring you a sense of peace and calmness, boosting your emotional well-being and your overall health. It can help carry you more calmly through your day and may improve certain medical conditions.

Its practice provides increasing levels of wellbeing and inner peace, allowing us to view life from a new perspective and solve our daily problems in creative new ways.

Breath meditation can calm you chattering mind in only a few minutes (at least one or two will do).

RULE 10 - **DEVELOP A WINNING MINDSET**

Only you have the power to decide how you react to specific situations, and whether or not you are able to control these reactions. In all cases, having a positive mental attitude is a crucial factor in determining whether or not you react properly and move forward in your entrepreneurial life.

Developing a winning mindset allows you to focus on what is working well in your business, your strengths and those of others, and the lessons derived from all your experiences, whether good or bad, empowering or crushing.

REMEMBER:

Now is the time to apply these Ten Golden Rules and build a winning mindset. And now is the time to take the precious road that leads to unlimited entrepreneurial success and financial wealth!

BY THE SAME AUTHOR
THE SECRET OF NOW SERIES

VOLUME 1
Living in "The Now" in Easy Steps

VOLUME 2
Buddhist Meditation For Beginners

VOLUME 3
Eckhart Tolle and Hinduism: Tales of Light

VOLUME 4
Christian Meditation in Easy Steps

VOLUME 5
Meditation in 7 Easy Steps

VOLUME 6

Stop Negative Thinking in 7 Easy Steps

VOLUME 7

Understanding Eckhart Tolle (2 x 1 Bundle)

VOLUME 8

Eckhart Tolle: His Life & Quest For The Power Of Now

VOLUME 9

Understanding Eckhart Tolle 2: In Search of The Power of Now

The Ten Golden Rules of Entrepreneurial Success

A. J.   P A R R

PUBLISHED BY:

GRAPEVINE BOOKS
Copyright © A.J. Parr 2019

Printed in Great Britain
by Amazon